CHASING MY TOMORROW

K. Zuba

Karen,
I am so blessed
to have such
an amazing and
supportive friend
and coworker!
Kim

ISBN: 1546765778
ISBN 13: 9781546765776
Library of Congress Control Number: 2017908036
CreateSpace Independent Publishing Platform
North Charleston, South Carolina

When troubles of any
kind come your way,
consider it an opportunity
for great joy.

-James 1:2

TABLE OF CONTENTS

"I Am"   vii

Chapter 1   Prelude to a Life Changer   1
Chapter 2   Night-Sweats, Needles,
              and a Need for Answers   4
Chapter 3   Sterile Field to Hospital Ward 6   10
Chapter 4   A Breath of Fresh Air   14
Chapter 5   Clinic Days   20
Chapter 6   MOPP/ABVD . . . ABCD, What?   23
Chapter 7   Golden Rules and Gang Busters   34
Chapter 8   From IV Access to
              Radiation Beams   39
Chapter 9   Tomorrow Fund Ball   44
Chapter 10   Teenage Love and Sunshine   47
Chapter 11   Introducing Amy-Jo: Cancer
              Superstar   50
Chapter 12   West Coast Dating   56

Chapter 13   From the Cliff Walk to the
             Clinical Setting   63
Chapter 14   The Real World   66
Chapter 15   Secondary Complications: Part 1   71
Chapter 16   Secondary Complications: Part 2   81
Chapter 17   Secondary Complications: Part 3   87
Chapter 18   Palliative Care   96
Chapter 19   Role Reversal/Papa Z:
             From Caregiver to Care Receiver   100
Chapter 20   Full Circle   109

Epilogue   115
Acknowledgements   117

"I AM"

I am a courageous girl who appreciates life.
I wonder when scientists are going to find a cure for cancer.
I hear my conscious telling me to do my best in everything I try.
I see the world becoming a better and safer place.
I want to have a successful medical career.
I am a courageous girl who appreciates life.
I pretend that I'm as well as everyone else.
I feel my guardian angel's hand on my shoulder.
I touch the sky when my attitude needs a lift.
I worry that I won't make it through my chemotherapy treatments.
I cry when I see people living in poverty.
I am a courageous girl who appreciates life.
I understand practice makes perfect.

I say, if you can't write something and sign it—don't say it!

I dream about helping everyone who needs it.

I try not to prejudge people.

I hope everyone will be equally accepted in the future.

I am a courageous girl who appreciates life.

—KZ, fourteen years old

CHAPTER 1

PRELUDE TO A LIFE CHANGER

The clock read two in the morning and the bed sheets were soaked yet again. Four times during the preceding weeks and almost robotically I had found myself in a new routine: school, homework, dinner, and soon after I'd fall asleep on the couch. Unfortunately, the remainder of my activity level was short-lived. Bed-soaking, body-shaking sweats woke me within hours of my head hitting the pillow, as images of a devil danced through my dreams. In a whisper, the distant words became clearer and clearer as I focused harder. Repeatedly, I heard the same message, *put up a fight*, but I didn't understand how significant the four words would become over the next few months.

At fourteen years old, many teenagers think they know it all, and I was certainly no exception to the rule. I was not considered a cool kid by any means (think crossing guard in the teacher's parking lot), but I had loyal friends, had proven myself academically, and was living a very promising and good life. I had been gifted with hard-working and dedicated parents, who were and still are, selfless in their ability to go without to provide abundance for their family. I had a younger carefree sister to torment, and a live-in grandmother to provide additional support, nurturing, and drama. My home was warm and always stocked with delicious food and desserts to share with friends and visitors.

Summers were spent at a small but quaint red beach cottage, owned by my grandmother, near a well-known family amusement park. During the summer prior to my life changing, I spent most days on the empty beach, throwing rocks, looking for the squirt of a native clam, and soaking in the water knee deep, digging for quahogs with my toes. Nights were spent walking along the cliff rocks, listening to waves, playing a game of Yahtzee, and popping corn in an old-fashioned popcorn machine—a treasure chosen from a local yard sale. Occasionally, we were treated to an afternoon on the nearby double-loop roller coaster, haunted house, and log-flume rides. Before long, freshman year of high school was about to begin, and the nervousness associated with transitioning to the much larger and frightening high school downtown set in.

The first few months of being a freshman were challenging but rewarding just the same. However, just months into the school year, days of absence and early dismissal began tarnishing my obsession for a near perfect academic record. I was constantly feeling under the weather. Repetitive visits to the pediatrician always resulted in the same diagnosis. I'd just about had enough of being told I had a viral syndrome that needed to run its course. Five visits later, I pleaded for confirmation via blood work. My reward came less than twenty-four hours later.

Laboratory testing confirmed the presence of Epstein–Barr virus. As quickly as the needle poked through my skin to get at my tainted blood, the hand that wrote the order also provided me with a free pass to be eliminated from further humiliating myself in my co-ed gym class. It was the best news I had received in quite some time. No more ugly gym shorts, bathing suits, and uncoordinated attempts at being athletic (outside of a dance studio, that is).

CHAPTER 2

NIGHT-SWEATS, NEEDLES, AND A NEED FOR ANSWERS

Friday April 19th is a date that has been permanently engraved in my brain. Weeks after my symptoms began, I again recall awakening in the early morning hours, my sheets drenched and wet clothes sticking to every inch of my shaking body.

Something was different this time. My mother had spent several nights before assisting with sheet changing and administering Tylenol and Motrin at all hours around the clock. This time, I awoke alone, pulled off my wet and cold shirt, and it seemed tighter almost. Slowly at first, and then more quickly, my hands scoured my neck. Yes, a dramatic change had occurred, almost overnight.

A hard mass, the size of an egg, was now embedded into the left side of my neck. At this time, the four words that had made their appearance multiple times in my previous dreams became clearer than ever before. I silently knew, at that moment, that my fight was about to begin.

Like any other teenager, I had been gifted with the ability to pretend things were okay, even in times where they were far from it. Such is the case on the morning of my new discovery. I chose to wear a black turtleneck sweater to cover any signs of evidence, and asked my grandmother to call in and have me excused from school for the day. My parents had left for work already that morning, kissing me on the forehead and wishing me a good day, per usual. Recently, I had been babysitting neighborhood kids who had come down with strep throat, and used that as the reason to head back in to see my doctor. An hour after my grandmother spoke to the school secretary, she escorted me to the pediatrician for the last visit of that kind.

The words my doctor spoke are still clear in my mind to this day.

"Call her parents out of work immediately," he sternly stated to my grandmother. As she excused herself to use a phone in his office as she had been instructed, it was my opportunity to turn and face him, vocalizing the thoughts that had lingered in my heart and mind all along.

"I have cancer."

As his eyes filled with tears, he looked aged and defeated. In his Russian accent, he managed to confirm my prediction and validate my fear. "It is highly likely that you do."

Even at fourteen years old, I was able to get in the final words, demanding that the information we shared was to remain between him and me until we knew if cancer was a sure thing. I left his office with instructions to meet my parents at a local surgeon's office for immediate consultation, and upon leaving his office for the final time as a *normal* teenager, I turned around once more, providing him with words of comfort. "Don't worry, I've got a good fight in me!"

And so, my story began.

Our meeting with the general surgeon was shorter than the time spent in the waiting room filling out paperwork. Initially, my pediatrician thought that a biopsy could potentially occur that same afternoon in the office setting. Given my age and the size and location of the mass, the specialist recommended I proceed with an excisional lymph node biopsy, in the hospital setting. As Friday afternoon office hours were quickly ending, we were instructed to return home, enjoy the weekend, and head to the local children's hospital for a same-day procedure the following Monday.

Over the next forty-eight hours, our home was surrounded by an influx of family members, friends, and acquaintances; the front door instantly became what seemed like a revolving door of curious guests, some sincere in their well-wishes and others who were somehow guilt-ridden into seeing the sick kid before her impending doom. (At least, that is what my fourteen-year-old brain thought at the time.)

Friends brought over movies to uplift my spirits. Even the Chippendales Revue was part of the attempt to incite laughter and calm my nerves. Comfort food and small talk filled the hours until I was to be introduced to my new life. This time gave me the opportunity of one more weekend to live as a normal teenager. Unfortunately, there wasn't anything normal about my situation. How does one prepare to be told she has a life-threatening disease? It's a question I often think of to this day.

The vacancy in my parents' eyes did not go without notice. The boisterous, outspoken, and even at times annoying qualities that I had learned to love and treasure were replaced with silent fear. Years later, I realized that they too had also done their research at the library and in medical journals, and were preparing a united front into accepting a potentially terminal diagnosis for their oldest child.

The early morning car ride to the hospital was life changing. Upon leaving my comfortable Cape home, I was able to kiss and hug both my ten-year-old sister and my grandmother, for the last time as a carefree high school freshman, one without cancer. My mother and father had accompanied me to the hospital and could stay with me until I was to be whisked off to the operating room. Clowns and video games were distractions for some, but not me. Luckily, a volunteer came over with some arts and crafts material, and I spent the next hour crafting beaded bracelets and trinkets of love for my family members and friends to treasure if I didn't make it out of the hospital alive. Dramatic, yes! I had been fortunate enough up until that point of my life to have only undergone minor surgery for tonsils and adenoid removal. The only other traumatic experience had been two separate occasions of braces, spanning three years, a whole saga in itself.

6:30 A.M. I've checked in and my insurance information has been verified.

7:00 A.M. We are waiting . . . but not so patiently.

7:30 A.M. I am hiding a mountain of fear while placing beads in a color-coordinated pattern on a string.

8:00 A.M. My name has been called and the count-down to my diagnosis begins.

CHAPTER 3

STERILE FIELD TO HOSPITAL WARD 6

The operating room is not an inviting place. The surroundings are cold and metallic. Sterility is important when dealing with life, death, and potential lawsuits. Almost instantly after shimmying from gurney to cutting table, I recall my body being overtaken by an unstoppable, teeth-chattering, and hair-raising chill—all of which happened in front of an audience of about fifteen strangers, some medical students I'm sure. Goose bumps replaced any of my exposed skin peeking out from the fashionable blue hospital attire, which included slippers with treads and a hairnet.

With the introduction of anesthesia, a burning sensation set off like a rocket through my vein and hot tears slid down my pale face. Instructions followed to start the count backward from ten, and by five my eyes were closed and I was dreaming of amusement park rides and beach days.

The next few days were a complete blur. I awakened out of sleep briefly only to fall back into a fog. Unbeknownst to me, a whirlwind of developments had occurred in the matter of days. Once the haze of medication and exhaustion lifted, I could make out a disheveled body asleep on what appeared to be a makeshift bed in the corner of my small private hospital room.

My eyesight became acclimated to the darkness, allowing a clearer picture of my father's features to come into focus. Something instantly seemed off. Within just a few days, my father appeared to have aged many years. New evidence of gray hair and an unshaven face helped to create the appearance of someone new and unfamiliar altogether. My mother soon entered the room, her facial features also drawn with dark circles and puffiness under her hazel eyes, the remnants telling of a good cry. She was carrying a cup of hot coffee for each of them, and when their eyes locked, suddenly words weren't necessary. I knew that it was time to talk.

Before any meaningful conversation could begin, a pleasant and energetic nurse arrived to check my vital signs, including my temperature, pulse, respiration rate, and blood pressure. She also asked me to rate my pain by either using a scale of one to ten or by pointing to a range of faces from happy to sad. My realization of extreme weakness quickly set in, as I required assistance to both sit up and then stand independently and walk to the bathroom, which was less than forty steps away. I recall cursing out loud, as evidence of my menstrual cycle took me by surprise. I was mortified. I seriously was embarrassed beyond belief. My body felt like a rag doll; shooting, stabbing pain radiated from my neck to my chest, and to make matters ten times worse, I had absolutely no privacy. I was living in my own version of teenage hell.

Panic set in as I began trying to figure out how to get out of bed without making a complete mess, all while trying to hold pressure on my neck to ease the aching and keep my developing body covered as much as possible. My dad graciously turned his face to the wall to provide the privacy I very much needed, and at that moment, my mother was also right on cue, holding the back of my open hospital gown closed. In a matter of seconds, we had worked as a team, a united front. It was then that I truly believed what my heart had felt all along: We could get through whatever laid ahead, together. And we would do so as a team when obstacles presented themselves, time and again.

CHAPTER 4

A BREATH OF FRESH AIR

A tall and handsome young physician entered my room on the sixth floor of the hospital. His eyes were bright and friendly. He had a little wave to his dark hair that paired well with a genuine smile and Italian complexion. It was early in the morning, and the sun could be seen through the large window adjacent to the bed. It was easily apparent to even a sick teenager that he was admired for his good looks, a favorite amongst the nursing staff and well respected on the unit by patients and families alike. As he put out his hand in introduction, I noticed his soft-spoken voice but also his strong presence, and instantly felt at ease. He was a new face to me, but by the greeting exchanged between him and my parents, it was evident that their paths had already crossed.

In a matter of seconds, my world was rocked, and not in the good way. This was not a typical introduction. This was real life and I was being introduced to my oncologist. He had come to discuss the results of my lymph node biopsy, the day procedure that turned into a multi-day hospital admission. He also provided a reason for my sore back and hip, explaining that the area had undergone a bone marrow biopsy during my time in the operating room. Multi-tasking at its finest! The results confirmed my diagnosis of Hodgkin's disease, a type of lymphoma. It took just a minute to register what had been told to me. Even though I had suspected all along a diagnosis of cancer, it was one thing to assume and another to have confirmation. Confirming my fears made me more vulnerable to an unpleasant outcome. In a not-so-polite manner, I raised my weak voice and asked the leader of my new team to get the hell out of my room.

He quickly and quietly stepped into the hallway just as I had requested. My father followed closely behind him, apologizing I'm sure for my abrupt and rude interaction. My eyes closed, and as I let my head hit the hard pillow, my favorite new music lyrics to a hip song on the radio filled my brain and gave me some strength to get it together.

I quickly asked for a pen and paper. Making a list always helped to calm my nerves and bring me back to focus on the task at hand. But first, I had questions needing immediate answers, and by writing them down, I could eliminate the emotion from the actual delivery. I first and foremost needed to apologize and ask the one with the answers to return.

"What is my chance of short-term versus long-term survival? Are we talking about controlling the cancer or curing it? What types of treatment options are there? Will I feel sick? Can I go back to school? And finally, why me? How in the hell did I get chosen to deal with this illness?" In fact, how is anyone chosen? Being diagnosed with cancer at any age is traumatizing. It is especially so during the teenage years when vanity is in and hair loss and bloating related to legal steroid use is not.

I was discharged home after a four-day hospital stay, during which most of my time was spent lying in bed trying to put on a brave face. Sure, I had visitors. Plenty of friends and family members came to share some time with me during the hours of 11:00 A.M. to 7:00 P.M.; to share small talk and prayers, and some occasional apologies for having to endure an anticipated hard road ahead. Plans were in process for further outpatient testing that would determine how extensive my cancer was and what treatment protocol I would be as-signed—so much for going back to school in time for the spring semi-formal dance and biology mid-term exam. It was time to bring on the bandan-na and wigs and say goodbye to the formal wear hanging in my closet.

Within a week, the handsome oncologist who I had not-so-nicely dismissed was once again deliv-ering news. The symptoms I had been experienc-ing for months, (and thought to be related to *just a viral syndrome*,) were actually signs of a poten-tially life-threatening disease all along. Hodgkin's disease can present with classic symptoms of fe-ver, night sweats, and weight loss. I had all three. Although causes are unknown, Epstein–Barr virus has been linked as a risk factor for developing this malignancy of lymphoid tissue. Initial staging of the disease is critical to therapy, which is why ev-ery part of my body had to undergo scanning. The mission of my new team was to search for cancer cells anywhere they could hide.

Deep within my chest, a tumor grew to be almost the size of a piece of fruit, likely over the preceding months. It was not palpable or visible from the out-side, but it was slowly trying to give me clues to its existence. Despite losing some weight, I was still on the overweight side. Diets be damned! The shortness of breath with activity I was experiencing was not just from lack of endurance. After reviewing initial staging tests, my case was discussed at Tumor Board, an interdisciplinary group made up of the best and brightest medicine has to offer. Chemotherapy and radiation were now planned for the next six to nine months.

Prior to my treatment being started, I was scheduled to return back to the operating room once again for a simple procedure. The cool atmosphere had already become familiar to my senses. Within an hour of checking in at the front desk and re-verifying insurance status, the infamous "count backward from ten" began. This time, I found myself awakening to another incision and mild discomfort. My neck was spared, and my chest wall became the newest victim. Chemotherapy was to begin within days; the length of actual duration unknown and dependent on response and tolerability along the way. Because of this, a decision was made to insert a PowerPort to allow easier access to deliver the toxic medications and draw blood, hopefully alleviating multiple needle sticks and sore arms.

A PowerPort is a small medical appliance that is installed beneath the skin, typically under the clavicle. A catheter connects the port to a vein. Under the skin, the port has a septum into which drugs can be injected and blood samples be drawn, multiple times if necessary. I had never been a fan of having a needle stuck in my arm—never mind my chest as a self-conscious developing teenager—and was not looking forward to what was ahead for me.

CHAPTER 5

CLINIC DAYS

An oncology clinic is a fascinating place. My first experience did not disappoint. With a waiting room approaching near capacity, two seats remained for my mother and I. My father had become a professional at checking in his children for events over the years—swim, dance class, karate—and was always at least fifteen minutes early to each activity. On time was considered late to him, given his extensive military service. The same held true at clinic that morning. As we found a seat and tried to relax, he took care of the rest of the details.

My mom had insisted that my sister, four years my junior, and I join her and her best friend during the hospital open house held only months earlier. Neither of us were thrilled to attend. A hospital tour and a free dolphin T-shirt had nothing on a few hours of people watching at the mall with friends. Nonetheless, we joined the adults and followed their lead through the bright halls of the freshly painted animal murals and scattered fish tanks. I remember gazing at the less fortunate patients, never dreaming life would shift only months later and I would become one. Yet here I was, trying to get comfortable in a hard and plastic blue chair amongst a crowd of ill people and their worried support groups, all staring into the same fish tank.

Several sets of eyes that I locked with appeared sad, but one set in particular had a kind and comforting vibe. This set, large and dark, belonged to a boy that appeared to be my age. Given his lack of hair, he didn't come across as a newbie, which made me both depressed and grateful at the same time. Maybe, just maybe, this trouble I was being introduced to would also bring me joy at some point during my life if I let it.

As my name was finally called, I gathered every ounce of courage and energy stored in my weak body and took a few steps ahead, asking my parents to wait behind. I was determined to remain calm and confident on the outside for as long as I could keep my walls up. I also wanted to prove to myself that I could be strong and get through the obstacles ahead even if my body was weak and changing drastically.

I soon met a cheerful middle age woman who took my temperature, weight, blood pressure and pulse. She then led me through a room to another woman, just as outgoing, who asked for a urine sample and drew a few vials of blood to check my blood counts and liver and kidney function. After about ten minutes, I rejoined my parents and we waited for the doctor to tell us exactly how I would be proceeding from that moment on.

This initial clinic visit became the first of close to one hundred during my active treatment phase. At each check in I was rewarded with a blue plastic card that displayed my name, date of birth, insurance information and provider. Little did I know then that these cards would become meaningful to my father- a collector of all things random. His request to me? To make sure the final one was made of gold. Challenge accepted.

CHAPTER 6

MOPP/ABVD . . . ABCD, WHAT?

Once all my testing was completed and my multidisciplinary team had ironed out my staging and treatment plan, I was assigned a combination chemotherapy regimen consisting of the acronym MOPP/ABVD. Initially, the letters thrown together sounded like a new language for my parents and I to learn. They quickly became known by my body and mind as the potent toxins responsible for my hair loss, bloating, mood swings, nausea, vomiting, and emotional and physical scars, all leading to a very distorted body image. Years later, this combination would be referred to again as the culprit for secondary complications affecting my twenties and early thirties, of which many nights were spent wondering *what if?*

The many nurses that I encountered in the oncology clinic were extremely personable and instantly likable. Their words and actions helped to ease not only my mind from racing but also my body from shaking. One of the fondest memories I have, still to this day, is of the initial meeting I had with the nurse practitioner assigned to the pediatric clinic. Beautiful on the inside as well as the outside, she quickly became a familiar face and sounding board, patient advocate, mentor, my living guardian angel, and friend all in one.

I was extremely self-conscious about my mid-chest port placement, so I was relieved to have a strong female presence assisting with my care. Sutures lining the incision were unfortunately starting to lift and pull apart, and as they did, it caused open gaps, messing with what I assume was supposed to be perfect closure. The gaps were large enough to slide the width of a pencil through. I know this because I actually tried doing it. Several Steri-Strips were placed in between the sutures that remained intact to re-attempt alignment. Time could not be wasted on waiting for the site to heal; chemotherapy was minutes away.

The first needle stick was torturous; more so because of my nerves than the actual pain itself. After being pre-medicated for nausea, a nurse arrived with several intravenous medications, one of which was as red as blood. My father nicknamed it my new fruit punch cocktail, and since that day, I have not been able to indulge in that sweet treat again. A distinct metallic taste filled my mouth, and a green apple Jolly Rancher eliminated it quickly. Only minutes later, my nerves had gotten the best of me, and I began dry heaving into the wastepaper basket. As tears streamed down my face, the floodgates opened, causing me to finally accept what was in store in the coming months. This fight was going to be more difficult than what I had originally anticipated.

I made it through the first of many sessions and was assisted from the car into the house by both of my parents. As I lay on the couch or in bed recovering, a pink kidney-shaped emesis basin was a permanent fixture at my side as well as my favorite lap dog Bonkers, who waited patiently to claim his spot. He was a terror to everyone else, but a ten-pound guard dog and lifesaver to me. Anti-nausea medication was my new best friend, although it threatened to break the bank for my parents. You see, each pill was extremely expensive when it first hit the market—and the generic brand was not yet available. I needed a pill every four to six hours for several days after treatment to control side effects. Although the cost of this was probably several hundred dollars for each session, I wouldn't know of the extra stress the expense caused my parents until years later, while looking back at all of their financial information. It just meant working more overtime for my dad when he felt comfortable with the extra hours, usually when I was feeling better and resting. There was nothing that man wouldn't do for anyone he knew, especially his family.

I must admit, it was nice to have my own personal assistants catering to my every need, screening phone calls, and taking messages. Initially, my visitors were assessed for possible infections, and the sterility of the hospital setting soon took over every aspect of my once normal existence. Hand sanitizer was a new decoration around the home, as were masks and gloves, if needed.

As the days passed by, I had been educated by many that my hair would begin to fall out. As a fourteen-year-old girl, I loved my hair, and this was one of the most difficult things to accept. Prior to my diagnosis, my mother paid for me to have a permanent. (Perms were totally in style during my teenage years; seriously I kid you not.) I had spent time trying out the newest and coolest hairstyles, but none of them included baldness. Approximately a week into chemotherapy, signs of imminent hair loss began: a few strands at a time in the shower, more on the pillowcase, and still more in the hands of anyone who touched my scalp. I became fearful of brushing my hair because—as silly as it sounds—losing hair gave me more of an emotional reaction than being told I had cancer. Many people recommended I consider shaving my head to avoid the daily grief of each strand hitting the pillow or accumulating in the shower drain. It was difficult to exchange my long locks for a shorter bob. That alone caused several hours of tears and an extremely generous but well-deserved tip for the hairdresser who assisted with my new style.

Fatigue began to set in rapidly, but I was determined to keep up with my schoolwork. Within days I was joined by several home school teachers on their off hours. English, math, and history lessons took place at my dining room table if I felt well enough to sit up and learn. Homework assignments were completed in the clinic waiting room prior to treatment, or while lying in bed following the completion of toxins, while I was recuperating.

As the days and then weeks passed, I began to feel isolated. My friends were wonderful and routinely called to check in on me or pop in for an actual visit here and there, but cancer began to change me. I no longer felt or looked like my old self and had a difficult time pretending otherwise. I started to feel more comfortable being alone and this scared me, as I always considered myself a people person. It was time to soul search.

After one month of chemotherapy, I did not resemble the girl that I once was. My face was rounded and blotchy thanks to the use of prednisone, an oral steroid and my personal new enemy. I was almost completely bald. Despite my very few and far between dark blonde strands of remaining hair, I still struggled to shave my head, despite my dad offering to do so daily. My eyebrows and even my eyelashes were missing, and my clear and easily bronzed complexion fluctuated between pale and pasty and red and blotchy. I looked like crap. As friends talked about upcoming field trips to the Boston Museum of Science along with managing busy social calendars, my focus was on whether or not I would require future hospitalizations for upcoming chemotherapy sessions and if my blood counts would remain high enough to allow me to be in contact with other humans at all.

Systemic chemotherapy continued over the summer months, and I fell into a new routine. I became more familiar with the pediatric oncology clinic, and the staff instantly became my extended family. I almost looked forward to each appointment, minus the nausea and vomiting that was sure to follow. My clinic visit each week was the outlet of familiarity and normalcy I craved, and it was fulfilled each and every time. I knew without a doubt that I could expect a set of vital signs, including a most dreaded weight, application of numbing cream to my port sight followed by a blood draw to check labs, a physical exam, mental check in, and chemotherapy every two weeks. Just as I had found acceptance, my family had also come to accept my new schedule and my new life. My dad, a federal employee and longstanding military man, adjusted his schedule so that he could take me to every medical appointment, as his job was much more flexible than my mother's. By doing so, he quite simply became my person. He wasn't just my dad, he was my advocate, my shoulder to cry on, my partner in crime, my shopping friend and sugar daddy, footing the bills for things that weren't needed but brightened my spirits nonetheless.

Just as I had striven to succeed in my academics, almost obsessively, as I had locked myself in my room once for getting a B+ instead of an A on a middle school report card, I also wished to have the same success in my medical quest—to kick cancer's ass quickly and permanently. My family, friends, and medical team believed I could do it, so I had no choice but to believe just as passionately myself.

At each visit to the clinic, I met new faces, and soon I became just another regular face amongst a crowd of ever changing people. After some time, I was no longer the new girl with cancer; unfortunately, that title continued to be passed on to many other children and adolescent patients.

Back to school shopping for the fall of my sophomore year was by far the most interesting and challenging for both my mother and I. Shopping did not only include clothing and shoes but also accessories for my newly bald head. At fifteen years old, as much as I tried to convince myself that I shouldn't be worked up over my complete hair loss, I continued to struggle. I still wasn't even comfortable "going bald" in my own home surrounded by my loved ones. Years later, going through graduate school and then while working as a physician assistant in palliative medicine, I've quickly come to understand the strength that accommodates hair loss at any age. And since then, I truly appreciate and feel that bald really is beautiful, and share that with all those individuals I come across in the same situation.

My parents, sister, and grandmother became used to my signature head gear, even at night, which was a black nylon Nike swim cap covered up by a local sports team baseball cap. They continued to voice their united request to take the gear off and allow my head to breathe. Each night, one of them would sneak into my room while I was asleep to remove the layers and air things out. This process continued for the entire length of my treatment. Nike swim caps were hard to come by after I cleared the shelves at local sporting goods stores.

Before school was scheduled to start, my mom and dad took me to a specialty wig store to purchase new hair. Although we came prepared with photos of my usual color, length, and style, I was not interested in participating. Choking back tears, I tried on several dark blonde wavy shoulder length wigs, securing them to my head by pulling the Velcro side taps tighter, and then proceeded to storm out yelling at my poor parents to choose one for me because I simply did not care. As a teenager, I didn't then realize the pain that scene must have caused my parents at an already unbearable time. As a parent, I get it now.

My new school schedule had been worked out between my parents, guidance counselor, teachers, and medical team. I would attend public high school four days a week, Monday through Thursday, and have chemotherapy treatments on Friday, allowing me the weekend to bounce back as much as possible prior to returning to class. This could only occur if my blood counts stayed in a safe range and if I were hypervigilant about my exposure to germs. I again no longer had to participate in gym class and instead worked on health-related material and testing. I could, however, do so from the bleachers, taking in the cute high school boys participating in each class, especially those that took place in the pool. Extra assistance and tutoring remained available to me and homeschooling was always an option if the schedule became too demanding to manage. If I required hospitalization and felt well enough, I could leave my room and attend classes offered throughout the day in the small hospital classroom. A teacher was always present and he or she could accommodate all grades. I craved normalcy and did everything in my power to continue at school, including making my infamous lists to keep me on track.

Of course, my special treats that came with being sick continued along the way. Before the nausea and vomiting set in, on our way home from every chemotherapy treatment, my very stylish father would still take me to his favorite clothing store, Eddie Bauer, and we would each leave with a new item to wear to our next scheduled hospital date. We would also grab something to eat for our family including my mom and my sister, if I could handle the smell of the food. Despite the warnings to not eat pizza or the steak and cheese grinder that I so craved, for fear of nausea and vomiting visiting, I often did so anyway and learned again that parents are usually right . . . I think we all became immune to the effects of vomiting as my family members each graciously took turns helping to clean up from the episodes that snuck up along the way, as their dinner often became cold in the meantime.

This included my younger sister, only ten at the time, who lost out on some of her own childhood despite our best intentions for that not to happen. Although my sister wasn't going through the actual toxic treatments, she unfortunately lived them just the same. She knew what a normal blood count was just the same as I did. She also knew how to screen possible playdates for early signs of illness.

At times, attention was often taken from her to deal with the acute issues striking me. Not at all fair but a reality nonetheless. Although I may not have realized it then or been mature enough to express my gratitude when the realization finally occurred, her sacrifices of time and attention contributed to my wellness and extended life. Cancer doesn't only change the patient. Cancer changes everyone that is brave enough to tag along for the ride. And I am so grateful that I had warriors in my army ready and willing to do so from the very beginning.

CHAPTER 7

GOLDEN RULES AND GANG BUSTERS

Be kind.
Show respect.
Treat others how you wish to be treated.

We are taught rules in our early stages of life, and often they are tucked away or slip through the cracks until somebody gets hurt. Upon returning to school, I attempted to resume some of my previous extracurricular activities, which included membership on student council. Our goal was to raise money for the less fortunate during the upcoming holiday season. Despite trying to fit in while doing something to help someone else, I was humiliated while sporting a new wig that was as close to real-appearing as we could afford. Some older popular kids in unison yelled out, "Why don't you take that money and go buy yourself some new hair?" The classroom soon erupted in laughter. I wish I could say that I was able to stand with my head and synthetic hair held high, but that was not the case. I quickly turned and exited the room in tears, and then was immediately comforted by good friends and teachers. Those measly thirteen words were harder than any surgery or chemotherapy I had yet endured. They have since given me the strength and compassion to treat others with the kindness and respect that we all deserve, no matter what their appearance may be.

For months leading up to the most anticipated formal dance of the 10th grade, my stomach was in knots. Yes, nausea was a constant from the ongoing chemotherapy. But even more nerve-wracking was the struggle for a bald and steroid-bloated fifteen-year-old girl to find a dress to cover the many new scars and healing physical and emotional wounds, and a date that would graciously accept me and all of the above.

It was around this time that my new social circle started to expand. Spending hours each week at an oncology clinic was something that I looked forward to, now for other more exciting reasons. Words were not always necessary there. Comfort came from seeing the same warm faces going through similar struggles—the same fears and the same tears, week after week. I was fortunate enough with assistance from my favorite nurse practitioner, child life specialists, and social workers to meet a group of teenagers that quickly became an important part of my life; a group that not only helped me find my faith, truly accept my diagnosis, and fight to overcome it, but also taught me to live each day to the fullest and truly enjoy the gift of each additional day granted, despite the less-than-optimal side effects along the way. This new social circle was made up of hard-core cancer warriors!

Many bald and beautiful males and females with variable diagnoses attended regularly with me. With the help of the Tomorrow Fund, we were able to initiate the first local teen support group of its kind. It was established that this group would meet on Friday evenings at the hospital, at least monthly. These nights quickly became an outlet to talk about the side effects of cancer treatment with others who understood the uncertainty of life expectancy coupled with the roller coaster of emotions, and physical and mental strains. There were certainly times that none of us wanted to talk about cancer but instead wanted to ignore the elephant in the room, and that was okay. By sharing our experiences, the weight from a single pair of shoulders was distributed to that of many. Daily with our parents, we were reminded that none of us were burdened in ways too unfamiliar from each other. Life experiences were shared, in hospital gowns and smiles, formal dresses and bald heads. Late-night phone calls, movies, bowling, love-life dilemmas, dinners with limo rides, and even a psychic visit filled some very special days.

Because of these new friendships, I was able to attend my winter dance with a fellow cancer fighter, a handsome teenage artist diagnosed with non-Hodgkin's lymphoma around the same time as my own diagnosis. I will always remember his kindness in accepting my invitation and his sweet mother's support and excitement for us. In that moment, the bloating and the wig didn't matter. Two friends, warriors, together in baldness, each on our own fight, danced the night away with over 100 healthy other teens including my close-knit group of girlfriends. As the DJ played the last song of the night, "Always and Forever" by Luther Vandross, I was overjoyed in my crushed green velvet dress and didn't even fidget when the neckline shifted downward to reveal ugly scarring. For the first time in a long time, I finally felt like I belonged in the high school setting, and it warmed my heart.

CHAPTER 8

FROM IV ACCESS TO RADIATION BEAMS

Excited to have gotten through nine grueling months of chemotherapy, I was finally being granted a break from the needle sticks and intravenous toxins! Radiation was the last step in my treatment plan, and I was scheduled for five days a week for four weeks. Simple, right? Not so much.

In order to start radiation therapy, more tests were required. Scan-xiety, anxiety one feels when preparing to undergo multiple diagnostic tests and procedures to determine the level of disease present in the body, quickly set in. A gallium scan; CT scans of the chest, abdomen, and pelvis; lab work; pulmonary function tests; and an echocardiogram were ordered. It seemed like I was busy hours a day preparing for the next course of treatment, in between juggling my schoolwork and extracurricular activities. I eventually found myself in hospital attire once again, lying on a cold stretcher getting permanent markings tattooed on my chin, behind my ears, and on my chest that would allow the technician to align the radiation beams to hit their target easily over the next month.

I wish I could say that I became comfortable with my radiation surroundings as much so as the oncology clinic, but that would be a huge lie. The radiation center was located in the dark and sketchy basement of the larger adult hospital that also housed a trauma center. In order to get to the clinic, one needed to take the elevator to the basement floor and follow the yellow dashed lines in the narrow and cold hallways reeking of odor. There were no bright lights, murals, tropical fish, or happy music to calm the nerves. It felt like a dungeon to me.

Although nausea was absent, it was replaced with an overwhelming sense of fatigue, severe skin burns and excoriations, and a dry mouth with intermittent lesions. My hair was still nonexistent, and I was not comfortable, often crawling out of my own skin. Because of the location of my tumor, the radiation target was in the worst possible place for this still-developing self-conscious teenage girl; my chest. Yes, I could hide my big bald head under my black nylon swim cap and wig, but I could not hide my chest, poor self-esteem, and body image from the daily grueling task of removing my shirt and lying still to be zapped with my arms and head locked into place with blue Velcro to assure that I didn't move even an inch. I absolutely dreaded each and every visit. I had to mentally prepare myself all day for the fifteen-minute session that awaited me after school was dismissed during the weekdays. Thirty days could not end soon enough.

While trying to save lives, we are often faced with decisions that need to be made almost immediately despite potential long-term risk factors. In my current line of work, I speak at length with patients and families regarding their personal goals of care. I spend time reviewing potential benefits and burdens of treatment options, reviewing advanced directives, and providing ongoing support in all areas. I'm sure my parents were offered the same education and support many years ago, but despite the risk of secondary complications, recommendations and preferences were in line with life-prolonging treatment—to do everything possible to extend my life. Treatment was with a curative attempt, all or nothing, and we were going for it all. Toxic chemotherapy came with side effects including infertility as well as chronic heart and lung disease. Radiation was so potent it could be responsible for secondary cancers at beam sites in years to come, including thyroid, breasts, and lungs. Time would tell. Although I am forever grateful for the gift of advancement in medicine resulting in my survival, growing older has certainly come with its challenges.

After completing a month of radiation treatments, the moment my family and I had prayed for and anxiously waited for ten long months had finally arrived. My scans were clear, no evidence of disease was found, and the same man that I had kicked out of my room at the beginning of my journey was back delivering the news. To make it even more memorable, I had a surprise of my own. I had spray painted one of those plastic blue cards, granted at each and every visit, a nice shade of glittering gold and happily presented it to my parents as a thank you. As my oncologist repeated the words we had been dreaming of hearing for so long, he set me free and challenged me to truly live my life and not be afraid of the journey or destinations ahead. Remission day is still the day that I internally celebrate year after year, reminding myself of where I've been and where I want to go in the future.

Although my body was grateful for the rest, relaxation, and detox from all of the previous poisons, mentally I was unprepared to return to my existing life. I didn't remember what that life was like. I had changed in the course of this process; how could I not? I again relied on the strength of my close friends at school who stuck by my life-altering process. I also found vigor in the group of friends that had become my social network inside and outside of the hospital walls. It was with the help of this support system and my immediate family that I continued to force myself to be present daily and actually look forward to and not fear what was in the cards for me.

CHAPTER 9

TOMORROW FUND BALL

Each year, the Tomorrow Fund hosts its largest and most anticipated fundraising event in the fall. Attendees are encouraged to wear formal attire, and the night consists of dinner, drinks for those of age, dancing, and a live and silent auction. Our teen group was invited to attend along with our parents to show how critically important it is to continue to support local families battling a diagnosis of cancer.

Our first formal event as a group was truly a rewarding experience and it is still remembered by my family and myself to this day. Bald really was beautiful as our group of seven teenage patients was called to take center stage. A standing ovation and applause that rocked the room soon followed. My hair had finally started to grow back in with dark and tight ringlet curls. The bloating had decreased with completion of steroids, and I actually felt comfortable in the public eye. Sporting a black form-fitting dress with a large slit, I felt beautiful and healthy. And so did my friends in their stylish dresses and handsome tuxes. It was a fun night celebrating life with some of the most important people in my life at that time. I know that my parents felt the same way as they looked on fondly at those they came to love and admire, not only for their strength, but also for their determination to live each day to the fullest without regret.

Some of the event highlights included watching guests outbidding one another during the live auction which raised astronomical funds towards helping children like our group in attendance and dancing the night away to an amazing band while feeling on top of the world.

The Tomorrow Fund continues to host this yearly event, with monies raised still benefiting every family of a child treated for cancer in the Tomorrow Fund Clinic at Hasbro Children's Hospital. This exceptional nonprofit provides direct financial and emotional assistance during both active and follow-up treatment, support to the hospital clinic, and outreach programs to inform the community about the effects of childhood cancer. The Ball is an event that I have been honored to attend many times:

during treatment, upon remission, as a survivor and as a medical provider. Each and every time has been special in its own way, but nothing can compare to my very first event which was just magical.

Each year more than 70,000 young adults continue to be diagnosed with cancer; six times the amount of cases in children, from newborn to fourteen. Children and young adult cancer survivors have a unique set of issues. They become survivors from the day of diagnosis and fortunately are living longer, but with an extended life expectancy comes potential secondary complications. Currently, one in every 100 college students is a young adult survivor, and I have no doubt that all could benefit from ongoing financial and emotional support. This statistic is alarming. We need to do better.

CHAPTER 10

TEENAGE LOVE AND SUNSHINE

It was the summer going into my senior year of high school, and I was finally getting a chance to feel and live like the teenager I had always dreamed about becoming. I continued to push myself in my day-to-day academics with the goal of graduating in the top ten students of my class. I was determined to get accepted, attend college, and focus my studies in biology and pre-medicine. I was also secretly determined to start dating, desperately wanting to experience the thrills of my friends' stories firsthand.

We met at a party in a friend's basement, and for the first time in my post-illness teenage life, a cute surfer-type tall athletic blonde, who had no prior knowledge of my crash course in chemotherapy, displayed an interest in me. First dates for many happen much younger than mine did, but I can't complain. It was nothing short of amazing to be out enjoying a simple activity without resembling sickness with someone so attractive and genuine. Things were light and exciting between us on the outside, but my internal struggle dragged on, of when and how I would explain my history. Rides through the local park, walks on the beach hand in hand, a movie date, mini-golf, and even an attempt at teaching me how to drive a standard vehicle, while neighbors probably shook their heads, filled our perfect days and weeks ahead. Several months after becoming an exclusive couple, I was scheduled to volunteer as a summer camp counselor for children with cancer and their siblings. It was with this upcoming multi-day event away that I gained enough courage to confidently share with him my struggles of the previous years. It was also during this time that I became a very fortunate young lady to have found a perfect gentleman to be my first boyfriend, one that was not afraid of my illness but who instead encouraged me to be myself, scars and all.

". . . after we started talking and going out and as we got to know each other better, I kept getting stronger feelings. You were all that I thought about. I couldn't be happier. After you told me about you being sick, I felt like I wanted to help. I felt bad about the whole thing. How could something so horrible happen to someone so innocent? Knowing you went through a difficult time, I wanted to be there for you always. It was then I knew I was falling for you . . ."

Like many first young loves, ours did not result in a happily ever after at the altar, but it absolutely did change my life for the better. Thanks to the immeasurable love, support, and acceptance that I received from this remarkably kind, compassionate, attractive, and giving individual, over several years of dating, my faith in love and friendship was fully restored, as was my self-esteem. I learned how to dream big and always search for the sunshine amongst the storms. And that's exactly what I've done with my life.

CHAPTER 11

INTRODUCING AMY-JO: CANCER SUPERSTAR

Not often in life do you come across at a young age someone as spontaneous, spunky, and ba-dass as my friend Amy. Introduced by cancer, and connected by the fight to survive anything thrown in our paths, our bond had become undeniable.

At just seventeen years old and as a high school senior, Amy was diagnosed with acute myelogenous leukemia. Nothing was going to stop my new pal, including chemotherapy, hair loss, or men unworthy of such a goddess. After her diagnosis, when others may have felt like their world of freedom and the excitement of heading off to college was being pulled away at lightning speed, Amy accepted the storm that awaited her and was determined to make a difference in the lives of those around her, simply becoming unforgettable to all she came across.

Instead of taking cooking and baking classes at the local culinary university as she had planned, she held them in her own kitchen with her new bald friends. She also held them in mine! Amy spent hours making chocolate lollipops to sell at the oncology clinic and children's hospital, with proceeds being donated to the very charity that was helping both her family and mine.

As she relapsed leukemia and was in need of a bone marrow donor herself, she volunteered as an advocate for the National Marrow Donor Program, helping to host drives in search of the perfect match for everyone in need, including herself. With mischievous eyes that could light up a room and a smile so infectious it was hard not to instantly join in, you could see her front and center on the television, manning the phones for many leukemia and lymphoma telethons.

During a period of remission, with her hair growing back in, she was finally able to attend college and live in the dorms, working toward pursuing her dream of becoming a pastry chef. Always ready for an adventure and a dance party, she truly enjoyed and made the best out of the time she was granted here on earth. She even moved into her own apartment outside of the city and worked in a local dance club, often stopping in unannounced to take a nap on my couch, with my sister or grandmother home to keep her company. She liked to turn heads, and she sure did grab the attention of her doctors when she displayed some permanent ink resembling the dolphin mascot of the hospital she came to love—and a few strategically placed piercings.

Amy also was known to pull some pranks—while visiting my dorm room in college, she outlined the shape of her body on the carpeted floor with detergent, so when my roommates returned after a night out on the town, the black lights illuminated a body that was not actually there.

Unfortunately, time was limited for her, and it affected all who came to love her. On July 26, 1999, after multiple relapses, a bone marrow transplant, and one hell of an amazing fight, Amy was called to her final resting place. Her parents allowed me the honor and privilege of remembering my dear friend at her funeral mass. The following is an excerpt from the eulogy I gave at the age of seventeen and a half, two years into remission myself:

"When love is strong and runs deep it pulsates with an energy that cannot be stopped, not even by death's grip. When our souls are connected and one departs from this world, the separation may seem final but in truth the relationship transcends time. Love, like a river, flows eternal and it embraces all those who swim in its stream. For those of us here to-day, we are in just that, a powerful stream. Our love and friendship for Amy and those closest to her have imprinted upon us in some mysterious ways.

"Invisible lines of connection link us all, and the heart always returns to its source. Once attachments are made they never truly disappear, but instead continue to live on in our thoughts, our deeds, our hearts, and our lives forever. Our eternal bond with Amy can only grow, and so it shall.

"It was Amy's power to illuminate others that brought us together several years ago. Faced with an illness and uncertain future, an unstable time for us both, we connected—at first as peers, and then as friends, and finally as soul sisters. Our times were shared with a special group of unique individuals. Together, our pain and sorrow diffused; by sharing our experiences with illness and life challenges, the weight was distributed from a single pair of shoulders to that of many, and every aspect of our lives promised to be more meaningful when shared.

"And share we did, in formal dresses and bald heads, in bandannas and bathing suits, in short skirts and attitudes, and most often in hospital attire amongst tears and smiles. Where trouble brewed, we were usually to be found. If gossip was collected, we were there to deliver the news and share it. Late night phone calls, thoughts, dreams, love life dilemmas, telethons, fundraisers, and chocolate making consumed some very special and unforgettable days. Many an afternoon was spent remembering our spirit with Oprah or catching up on our favorite soap opera storylines. I admired Amy's ability to be such a free spirit despite her illness; her inspiration and constant encouragement helped mold me into the person I am today.

"Amy truly lived for the moment. I honestly believe she was fulfilled by her own sense of adventure. At times, she searched like many for her true identity, and when it found her she was nothing shy of being a dedicated athlete, a fantastic chef, and a beautifully compassionate person. With spunk and wit, she gained the respect and attention of all those around her. She inspired many to be true to themselves, and after all, she set an incredible example. Amy has left footprints on my heart that will forever remain.

"We think there is always a tomorrow, so why expose our feelings today? Why risk being vulnerable? Why take the chance? Because today what we love, what we feel, what is real is what we have. Tomorrow it may all change. In closing, I encourage you to live like Amy. Do not walk in front of anyone, as they may not follow. Do not walk behind, as they may be too weak to lead. Walk beside them, hand in hand, and be their friend. After all, the reward of love and friendship is in itself. Amy, walk with Jesus.

Cry, laugh, share, guide, and most of all, smile down upon us."

Years after Amy's death, I'm still blessed by her strong presence in my life during some of the most difficult of days. A simple song on the radio can spark some vivid memories. Amy's parents have also continued to be by my side, along with my own, to share in life's milestones; they were present as I graduated college, crossed a half marathon in honor of her birthday with a wonderful group of my friends, attended my wedding, and have helped to celebrate my survivorship and many blessings each step along the way. I am beyond blessed and forever grateful.

CHAPTER 12

WEST COAST DATING

I was fifteen years old when cancer introduced me to the person that would become my reason for being during my early college years. Introduced at one of our Friday night teen group meetings, an outspoken tall blonde with a sparkle in his eye (do I have a type here?) undergoing chemotherapy treatments for leukemia quickly grabbed my attention. He appeared animated and carefree, two qualities I was deficient in and drawn to just the same. Our friendship grew over the next two years, spending time together in many group settings having pizza, catching a movie, enjoying holiday parties, and even attending a formal event for the Tomorrow Fund. During these outings, our families blended, enveloping us in their support, both during and after treatments.

After reaching remission and before graduation from high school, I was asked to accompany my friend to one of his semi-formal dances. He was a year behind me in school. Although my hair had grown back and I looked a lot like my old self pre-treatment, I had changed. My confidence level was lacking, but in his presence, I felt comfortable, and ultimately ended up having a great time.

The summer prior to leaving for my freshman year of college, he and I spent a night out on the town, after he finished his high school mascot duties and I finished a shift of retail work. We celebrated friendship and health, as we were both considered to be cancer free and thriving. As usual, our time together was upbeat and fun—grabbing dinner and completing the night visiting a local psychic for a palm reading (my idea, despite knowing that our parents would probably be less than thrilled).

During this visit, the psychic revealed that within a short period of time, things would drastically change for both of us. Life would be thrown a curve ball, testing both his health and our faith, but ultimately with support, including mine, he would overcome the ordeal a stronger person. Bright times would again be found by the following August. For two people that had already overcome so many obstacles, the news was shrugged off by both of us. The night ended with deep conversation, listening to music, ice cream, and a casual goodnight hug and kiss with promises to keep in touch and meet up again soon.

During my first weeks as a freshman in college, I struggled to find my niche. My first roommate and I were complete opposites, and after forty-eight hours, I found myself packing up and lugging my belongings across campus, with the help of some of my high school friends' muscles, to a new room and new adventure. I usually spoke to my parents and boyfriend multiple times a day. I also spoke with my friends often, as we attempted to help one another via phone and e-mail get accustomed to being away from home and each other. These were the days before Skype and prevalent social media. My teen group friends were no exception, and I made it a priority to remain an active part of group meetings.

While studying one evening for an exam, I received a phone call from my parents letting me know that my dad was on his way to visit with some unfortunate news to share. My dorm was about an hour and two bridges away from my parents' home, so for either of them to drive randomly on a weeknight, I knew the news to be delivered was going to shake me. My mind initially was focused on the health of my elderly grandmother, but the truth was even more shocking.

My dear friend whom I had just seen weeks earlier had gone to clinic for a routine appointment, and blood work revealed concerns for a relapse of leukemia. Immediate talks included aggressive treatment, including a bone marrow transplant.

The curve ball was thrown, and there was no looking back.

Our mutual group of friends met at his house amongst other members of his close network to provide silent and vocal support over the next days. Life was changing drastically for this family, and I felt the strong desire to be present and do everything in my power to help ease the tumultuous journey ahead, if that were even possible. To be able provide the level the support I wanted to give and maintain my studies with an eventual goal of medical school, I ultimately and with a heavy heart ended the relationship with my boyfriend of almost two years. I also became less present in many other of my former friendly relationships, and avoided the typical college scene altogether.

My feelings grew with each and every phone call, text page, date, letter, and tearful conversation leading up to his departure across the country for a life-saving bone marrow transplant. Our connection ran deeper than I had ever experienced with another person. I was willing to quickly give up all that I had worked so hard to achieve, including my college studies and activities, to be by his side. He quickly became my reason for existence, my next breath, my obsession. I was all in, emotionally, physically, and spiritually. I had again been introduced to young love and felt that I had met my soul mate and life-long partner, at such a young age, given our experiences with life threatening illness.

The effects of the initial induction chemotherapy were brutal, ravaging his once strong body with the risk of death at any given time, and although I was in close contact with his parents, brother, and best friend, it was difficult to go on with my life thousands of miles apart, always wondering what was going on across the country in that hospital room. Some of my fellow college peers were out partying, having fun, and partaking in random hook ups, while I was drawn to the phone, waiting for any message that would allow me to breathe a sigh of relief for more time, one more visit. We used old-fashioned pagers, sending numerical messages to decode—143, 831, etc., and receiving one of these messages became my Friday night fun. With the help of both of our families, I was lucky enough to leave school often for a long weekend and during semester break to fly to his bedside, either alone or with his brother and best friend.

I had fallen graciously into my role by his side as his partner, and thrived on being able to provide him with care, hope, love, and small comforts. The more time we spent together, the deeper I fell for him. He truly became my reason for living during that time, and at moments he consumed me. Our bedside experience, patient and caregiver, was a factor that ultimately led me into pursuing a career in palliative medicine. I spent many a night curled up beside him in his hospital room, assisting with some basic caregiving when he let me—layering clothing due to a sudden chill, being a steady arm with transfers to the bathroom or small walks, all while praying for our future together. I was even granted the honor of being at his side with his immediate family as the marrow of a generous live-saving donor arrived and was transfused. After 100 days in isolation, during a warm and sunny summer month, just as the psychic predicted almost a year before, he was allowed to start the next chapter of his life.

Although our connection was strong and our experience together unlike most, we were young and ultimately headed in different directions. Our relationship was strained during the school year with multiple demands, distance, and typical young-adult drama. As his health improved and he could set sail into a promising future, my caregiving role was no longer needed. Ultimately, our relationship ended, and the stages of grief set in for me. I would sob as a familiar song played on the radio, and even became visibly sick months later after randomly seeing him with someone new at a movie. It took me many years to find peace and closure within myself, many years to move on and open myself up to the journey that was ahead. And once I gave myself permission to do so and find happiness again, quite the journey was in store for me!

This person, his family, and his closest friend came into my life for a reason, and I am forever grateful for the bond that we created and the love and experiences we shared. Many years later, one of these friendships would prove to come full circle, at the most difficult time of my adult life thus far, bringing me closer to God and enveloping me with spiritual peace.

CHAPTER 13

FROM THE CLIFF WALK TO THE CLINICAL SETTING

I spent the remainder of my college career focusing almost solely on my academics, aside from daily walks along the water on the world-famous Cliff Walk in Newport, Rhode Island, and the occasional party or bar crawl courtesy of my friends and roommates. I dated here and there, and thought at one time that a particular person and I were exclusive after months of seeing one another, only to find out that he was also "exclusively" seeing many other people at the same time.

Soon to be graduating with a degree in biology with a concentration in pre-medicine studies, I had a decision to make. I had proven to myself that I could maintain my academics amongst curve balls, even receiving the top honor microbiology award in my graduating class. It was time to complete applications that would soon determine what would happen if I were not to enter the working class just yet. Initially, I had been set on working for a year in the laboratory to focus on research, and then I planned to apply to medical school. After talking it over with my parents, I decided to change course. I started immediately working toward a minimum requirement of clinical hours, choosing to take a class as a certified nursing assistant. I also shadowed local physician assistants in different specialties, and took the necessary standardized tests in hopes of becoming a certified physician assistant (PA-C). I applied to only one program and left it up to fate.

My expectations of getting accepted into PA school right out of college were slim to none. The average age of those in the graduating class before I was due to enter was at least six years older than I was at that time. In addition, they had real-life experience, and not just an undergraduate degree with part-time work at the local Gap and nannying for twin two-year old girls, teaching them ballet moves in pink tutus with handfuls of Goldfish crackers. Nonetheless, I was determined to prove my desire to work in this demanding and exciting field, and made sure I worked every last clinical hour required to apply, and wrote a kick-ass essay.

My father has always been an absolute saint. He awoke at four in the morning to accompany me to my interview several hours away. He ironed my suit in a way only a military man can, and then handed me a cup of tea for the road. He calmed my nerves the entire time, telling me that he believed that I could do anything that I put my mind to. He sat in the car for two hours as I answered question after question about my life's goals, challenges, and fears. He handed me Kleenex on the ride home when I was sure I flubbed my chances of getting in. And he made sure I got back to Newport, Rhode Island the same night to catch the senior cruise that I had been looking forward to, with my friends and roommates waiting for me to get the night started. Just as graduation weekend ceremonies were due to begin, it was he that handed me my acceptance letter and made sure I had everything needed for the road ahead.

CHAPTER 14

THE REAL WORLD

Getting through twenty-seven months of gradu-ate studies and clinical internships, both local and as far away as New Mexico, was exhausting and rewarding just the same. I was able to accomplish some pretty amazing and scary things with the best people! I spent a total of ten weeks at a federal prison, first practicing internal medicine at inmate sick call, and then working with a specialized psychiatry team learning as much as I could about treating mental illness (all while battling frustration along the way due to our lack of much-needed supports in this country). I then spent five weeks living in the emer-gency department of a rural hospital in New Mexico. I will never forget the night of a horrific bus accident carrying a team of female high school athletes and the disaster call alarming us to prepare for the arrival of those needing immediate attention. As the last of the victims were sutured, stabilized, or air-transferred, I was physically and emotionally drained.

My good friend and I had planned to take two days off during the entire block of our clinical time to fly to Las Vegas, and wouldn't you know, we both spent our time on the strip searching for bathrooms instead of a winning at blackjack tables due to a horrible gastrointestinal virus. It's comical to look back on years later, but boy was it frustrating at the time. Decked out in cute outfits and brown bags to serve as emesis basins, we were quite the sight. Although we avoided the Vegas buffets and didn't take advantage of the free alcohol the casinos had to offer, we did manage to make it to a Cirque du Soleil show that we had gotten tickets to, although to be honest, I think I slept through most of it.

Rounding out my clinical journey, I can say that I thoroughly enjoyed my time spent at a pediatric clinic in New Hampshire, several internal medicine and family practice offices, as well as a local Ob-Gyn practice, in both the office and hospital setting. However, my time in the operating room of a busy city hospital as part of the general surgery team was time that I dreaded day after day for five weeks straight. The only time I felt at complete peace was when I cared for veterans undergoing treatment for cancer, as their experiences had mirrored my own in many ways.

During the final six months of my program, I met the man that would become my husband. Again, I faced the challenge of when to expose my health baggage, and feared that it would instantly strain our early and casual relationship, as we were simply dating and not exclusive. However, I was older and wiser by this time (so I thought), and did not want to grow a deeper connection with him without sharing the knowledge of potential health complications I may face in the future. I felt that I needed to be completely honest and up-front, so he could reflect on the information I provided and then decide for himself whether or not I was worth taking a risk on.

My health struggles quickly became apparent when my suitor planned a hiking date in the Blue Hills, in Massachusetts. I was so not prepared for a day of outdoor adventure—he left out important details about dress code and weather conditions— but I was willing to make the most of our time together. (It was hard to come by with my clinical responsibilities and travel every five to six weeks, juggled with his full-time employment in the busy city.) After climbing the mountain in my black pants and dress shoes, my typically quiet friend asthma decided to make a brief appearance until we returned to the car, which housed my pocketbook and inhaler. Our date ended quickly after grabbing a coffee on the road, one that I paid for as he just so happened to leave his wallet at home, and as I drove back to my apartment over an hour away to start preparing for an upcoming examination and clinic hours, I was convinced that it was the last time that I would be meeting up with him. I also shared this with my best girlfriends who were waiting for details of our date.

I was wrong. We continued to keep in contact by phone and e-mail several times a week, growing a friendship and a solid foundation. We did not initially see one another often due to scheduling conflicts, but when we did, we had a good time and I always looked forward to the next. As our relationship continued to blossom, and before the physical aspect could advance, I had to share my past. After several surgeries, my body was a landscape of scarring, and I had trouble looking at myself in the mirror, never mind exposing my body and opening my heart again to someone new after suffering such a heartbreak only years earlier.

With the encouragement of my support network, I was reminded that I had come a long way and was worthy of happiness. They reminded me that I had nothing to be ashamed of and encouraged me to become as confident on the inside as I appeared on the outside. And then there were times that I could clearly make out Amy's voice telling me to find someone that was interested in what I had to offer and who not only wanted to be with me, scars and all, but couldn't live without me.

It just so happens that I had found that person when I wasn't really looking. And after a little more than a year of dating, he got on bended knee, in my favorite beach town with the sound of waves surrounding us, a lighthouse in the distance, and asked me to spend my forever with him.

We married less than a year later surrounded by those that held a special place in our life together. Supporters from all aspects of my health care journey were present to celebrate us and made the occasion even more memorable. Although our honeymoon flight was briefly delayed and rain and hurricane winds welcomed us to Bermuda, these challenges only symbolized to me that we could continue to weather whatever storm came our way.

CHAPTER 15

SECONDARY COMPLICATIONS: PART 1

Not even a year into our marriage and my biological clock was seriously starting to tick away. I had always dreamed of completing my family through birth and adoption, if blessed enough to be able to do so. Although my husband preferred to wait until he felt the timing was right, I felt differently. I didn't need our finances to be more secure or our home remodel projects to be completed. I could have given up the luxury of being able to travel more freely, without restrictions or responsibility for a little longer, in exchange for a promise to try adding to our family. I had been replaying conversations with my specialists throughout the years in my mind—those that cautioned me of infertility as a secondary complication from prior chemotherapy, with anticipation that I would soon develop premature menopause. I was no longer on birth control, as I was fearful that the side effects would result in a blood clot, or even worse, cancer.

After months of abnormal periods and no signs of pregnancy, I sought further guidance from my gynecologist. She agreed to run baseline blood tests to check my thyroid and hormone levels given my prior history. When they returned, my results were delivered in her office and not in an examination room, as testing revealed that I had poor ovarian reserve—basically compromised ovarian function making a natural pregnancy difficult to achieve, but not impossible. I was referred to a fertility specialist and began researching adoption agencies at the same time.

My meeting with the fertility specialist was less than promising. After reviewing my history and testing results, she asked me if I had a family member or friend that I would consider asking to be our egg donor. I left the office discouraged. Instead of scheduling a follow up appointment at the time of check out, I requested more time to consider not only my personal feelings about options discussed including a trial of fertility medications, egg donation, and the option of hiring a surrogate, but I also needed time to present the options to my husband, allowing him to collect his own thoughts, and then discuss our hopes and plans for a future together.

Maybe six weeks later, I felt fatigued and waves of nausea began to affect me as I provided patient care in a nursing home setting. After weighing the options of excitement and disappointment, I finally let myself take a pregnancy test, and slowly watched a plus sign appear. I immediately had to go out to the local drug store and purchase several more, all different brands, as I couldn't believe what I was seeing. I called my doctor the next day and scheduled an appointment. Blood work confirmed that I was in fact pregnant, but within a week of elated happiness, I began to bleed, and miscarriage was imminent.

It was then that I came to realize that this was His plan and not mine—that God's plan was better than my dream. My relationship with my husband was strained as I was hurt and angry, and my emotions were all over the map. I wasn't pleasant to be around until I came to accept what occurred. And once I did and we figured out how to support one another, based on our needs at that time, things started to improve.

Can you believe that two months later, as I went back to the fertility specialist laboratory for repeat hormone levels prior to contemplating starting a fertility drug, that my blood work read pregnant, again? I had been experiencing abnormal bleeding for days and never expected that my blood work would confirm a pregnancy; instead I was worried about the possibility of a malignancy or menopause.

The physician cautioned me that bleeding was not a promising sign for a healthy pregnancy, but gave me an appointment for an ultrasound in the coming weeks. During the ultrasound, we could see and hear our child's heartbeat, although it was much slower than average and I continued to bleed on and off. Again, she cautioned that this pregnancy would likely result in a miscarriage and discussed the role of a dilation and curettage procedure. I had one done months before, and was not interested in pre-planning a potential return to the operating room, so I declined, despite her adding that she had only been wrong a handful of times, and remained concerned that this pregnancy was not going to be a viable one. It was then that I elected to return to the care of my primary medical team and pray for the best. Despite being nervous to travel in the midst of the unknown, we made the best out of an already planned trip to Walt Disney World, and had an excellent time. After arriving home, I had another appointment scheduled, and looked forward to a repeat ultrasound. My excitement was short lived, however, when bleeding resumed and our child's heart rate was no faster than it had been weeks earlier.

Life around us continued with our demanding jobs, family, and home responsibilities. We decided to take things one day at a time. Those single days turned into weeks and then into months. And I cherished every day that I remained pregnant.

Halfway into the pregnancy, around twenty weeks, a regularly scheduled pre-natal ultrasound was concerning due to an abnormality. Typically, an umbilical cord has two arteries and one vein. However, our child's cord had just one artery and one vein, a condition known as a two-vessel cord. This condition came with increased risk for birth defects including heart, kidney, and spinal defects; slower-than normal fetal growth; pre-term labor; or stillbirth.

Higher resolution scans were ordered including a fetal echocardiogram and more genetic testing, and I found myself adding more frequent medical appointments to my already overly scheduled calendar.

Although our child's growth was slower than normal in comparison to others, he was still growing and his heartbeat remained steady. That's all we could ask for.

Things were status quo until they weren't. After leaving a routine pre-natal appointment and arriving to work to hold a family meeting for a patient with advanced dementia and failure to thrive approaching the end of her life, I felt a sudden gush of liquid and then noticed a large amount of bleeding seeping onto my white coat. It was almost six and half weeks prior to my due date, but I immediately knew that things were happening quickly.

It took me over an hour to get in touch with my husband who was in and out of meetings despite numerous phone calls and text messages, and during that time, I returned to the doctor to confirm what I already expected to hear—it was go time. There was no bag ready, the paint colors I had chosen for a perfect nursery were unopened, and I was supposed to be attending my ten-year high school reunion later that weekend. But I had become accustomed to being thrown a curve ball.

Hours after arriving to the hospital as a family of two, we were introduced to the little warrior who would make us parents. At just shy of four pounds, he was quickly whisked away to the neonatal intensive care unit after we caught our first glimpse of him. I had given birth to a miracle and I felt confident that he had inherited my genes to put up one hell of a fight. And that he did!

After a few weeks in the hospital, he passed a car seat challenge test and was given the green light to come home with us. This joyous day was even more special, as it would have been Amy's thirtieth birthday.

The following is a note from mother to son to help answer any questions and doubts that may arise in the future, if I'm not here on earth to personally answer them for him:

My dearest C—

You are the greatest blessing that I have ever been granted. I have loved you more that life itself from the moment you were just a dream. My love and gratefulness expands exponentially by the day, although some days are way more challenging than others. You continue to make me so proud. As you know, when mommy was a teenager, I was diagnosed with cancer. Nannie and Papa brought me to all of the best doctors available to help me get better. With God's hand and their help, I am still here with you today.

One of my biggest struggles, years after my illness, was trying to make my dream of you become a reality. Daddy and I tried for quite some time to have a baby. After almost a year and a half of disappointment, a fertility specialist ordered blood tests, confirming that my chances of actually conceiving a child without assistance were extremely poor; this was related to the side effects of the medicine I had received all those years ago, to make me better. Soon after the testing was complete, we discovered that I was pregnant. Unfortunately, within weeks an ultrasound confirmed a miscarriage, and grief took over.

A little more than two months later, I again became pregnant, this time with you. Our pregnancy journey was a bumpy road from the beginning with a lot of complications. You gave us quite the scare on multiple occasions. Our faith was repeatedly tested, but we remained hopeful throughout each episode despite the specialists that were required along the way. Almost six and a half weeks prior to your due date, while I was at work in the nursing home on the Friday before Labor Day weekend, you made your appearance. At just shy of four pounds, as you were struggling to take your first breaths and requiring immediate assistances, my nerves were again tested but my heart was so full. I was instantly in love and afraid of losing you at the same time. You were given the name Camden to represent the winding road of our journey, and then whisked away to the NICU where you required twenty-four-hour care, breathing assistance, bilirubin lights, and many more interventions.

Daddy and I were finally allowed to hold you days later, and our hearts could not have been more content. Day by day we learned how to feed you through a naso-gastric tube, and then by syringe. A few weeks after your birth, after multiple successes, including the official car seat challenge, we were allowed to bring you home on what would have been Auntie Amy's thirtieth birthday. As one of your guardian angels, I believe she helped lead you home to celebrate on that special day! She always did love a good celebration and pastry!

As you get older, please don't ever for a single moment doubt my love for you. I want to give you the world and will continue to try to do so every day of my life. As you have grown up, you have frequently asked why we have not given you a sibling to share your days with. My sweet Cam—I want you to know that you are truly my miracle child. If God leads us to help another child in the future, I have all the confidence in the world that you will be an amazing big brother, as you already are an amazing big cousin, friend, and teammate to many. You are an absolute treasure to our family. It is a privilege to be your Mom.

All my love always,
Mom

CHAPTER 16

SECONDARY COMPLICATIONS:
PART 2

By thirty years old, I had become a professional with preventative testing. I had spent the last sixteen years of my life being scanned, poked, and prodded. I was constantly worried about getting a second cancer diagnosis and wondered how it would affect my family of three. I was familiar with yearly mammograms and ultrasounds since the age of twenty-five, and always prepared myself for being told of an abnormality, especially with the heightened risk from previous radiation exposure during puberty. I went to the doctor for breast concerns, as I was having intermittent breast pain and thought that I had felt a lymph node under my arm, and with tremendous thanks to a highly educated and informed provider, I ended up with an order not just for the usual breast-related screening, but also for a thyroid ultrasound. According to the doctor, radiation beams had been directed in that area as well, elevating the risk of yet another form of secondary cancer.

It was the day after Thanksgiving, and instead of eating leftover turkey sandwiches, my sister's favorite chocolate peanut butter pie, or starting my Black Friday holiday shopping with thousands of others, I sat reading an outdated *Vogue* magazine, waiting to be called into the diagnostic wing of the medical center. My good 'ole dad sat in the car with my sleeping two-year-old. Within minutes, my name was being called and I was brought back to undergo an ultrasound of each breast as well as my thyroid gland followed by a diagnostic mammogram. An hour or so later, I was discharged with instructions to await a call from my primary care provider with results. No call was considered good news, followed by confirmation via letter in snail mail form. Papa and his boy had enjoyed their time together, eating Goldfish and listening and dancing to music in the car, while waiting for me to come out.

Within twenty-four hours, a call came from the imaging center and then my primary care office, and boy was I shocked. I expected to be told I had a breast abnormality that would require me to come back for additional images. My mother had something similar in prior months, and my paternal grandmother had died in her early fifties of complications related to breast cancer. I expected with the addition of the radiation exposure, the time clock to this type of diagnosis had to be ticking. Luckily, my breast ultrasound and mammogram were clear; however, the thyroid ultrasound was not. A large solid mass was found, suspicious for malignancy. Biopsy was the next step.

I didn't have to wait a weekend this time to prepare myself to be told that I may have a cancer. Just twenty-four hours later and I was off to the hospital outpatient interventional radiology center for biopsy. I was given the option for local sedatives prior to the procedure with the risks of sedation, nausea, and confusion clearly outlined. I was also told that the actual biopsy itself would be quick, so I decided to grin and bear it without medications, so I wouldn't be sedated when I returned home to my young child later that day.

Draped in sterile blue with just my neck exposed, my eyes were full of tears and thankfully hidden from the medical team. My nerves were finally getting the best of me. One expected poke of the needle and sample led to five, then nine, and finally twelve—although twelve felt like a hundred. Each jab into my neck felt worse than that of the previous;

the pressure of the needle was unbearable, like an ice pick chipping away at a glacier, piece by painful piece. I endured all of this while I heard the same phrases being voiced by the medical professionals that were already on replay in my head: "Hodgkin's disease as a teenager, history of mantle radiation, solid mass, sixteen years later."

Returning home sore and drained, with a pressure bandage in place on my neck, and an attitude ready to beat the odds if I needed to, I could only wait for the answer that would lead me to the next phase of my journey. Pathology results returned within seventy-two hours, and unfortunately were not as clear-cut as I would have preferred. A follicular mass was identified; the only way to be sure it was not cancer was to remove it, and have pathology further examine the entire specimen. The answer in my mind became quickly clear: I wanted the entire thyroid gland removed; a total thyroidectomy was the only choice I'd accept. With the help of my dedicated oncologist and friend, the one I had tossed out of my room during my teenage years, I was referred to an endocrinologist and surgical oncologist to review the films and biopsy report. He even took a minute from seeing his own patients to check in on me during this consultation and it made a world of difference, as he has always had a calming effect on me during the most unsettling times. I was given the option of having a partial thyroidectomy, which would remove the mass and buy time while waiting for the final pathology report. If cancer cells were present, I would need a second surgery to remove the remaining lobe of my thyroid gland. I chose to remove the entire gland up front knowing that even if cancer cells were not present, and total removal would require daily thyroid hormone medication for the remainder of my life, at least I would have the peace of mind that I had beaten the odds once again.

Surgery was scheduled for three days prior to Christmas. Although I was scheduled for the first surgery of the day, my time was bumped back several hours due to an emergency. And what we anticipated to be a quick twenty-four-hour hospital stay ended up double that thanks to the wonderful side effects of general anesthesia and my body's poor tolerance to them. Teeth-chattering chills, intractable nausea, and vomiting held me prisoner to my uncomfortable hospital bed in a semi-private room. Never, in all of my ill encounters, had I experienced the feeling of crawling out of my skin so badly. However, the surgery was successful, and my entire thyroid gland and one parathyroid gland were removed. Scarring was minimal thanks to the expertise of a wonderful surgical team. Thankfully, my husband and family were amazingly supportive, and I was able to enjoy the holidays from my couch, surrounded by my loved ones and my special two-year-old little boy.

The results returned less than a week later and were negative for cancer cells. The large solid mass was that of a follicular adenoma, and thankfully benign. My incision was on its way to being well healed and considered just another battle scar on my road-mapped body. I was informed that the incredible fatigue that had taken over my body the week following surgery, making me feel like I was hit head-on by a truck, was due to severe hypothyroidism. Once I started on the right synthetic regimen, I was back to my old self. Ten days later, I returned to work full time and was more than ready to continue making a difference in the lives of those compromised by chronic and debilitating illness.

CHAPTER 17

SECONDARY COMPLICATIONS: PART 3

Seven years after my first yearly scheduled mammogram, I received the call that I had been dreading. I was asked to return for repeat imaging given an area of concern on my right breast. Interestingly, this was the same breast that I had sought attention for earlier due to discomfort. I made the appointment and cleared my schedule to allow for me to be able to get there from work and back in time for daycare pick-up. Unfortunately, repeat imaging was inconclusive and I was asked to again return, but this time for a breast MRI.

Given my prior experience with repeat testing and ultimately favorable outcomes, I continued with my day to day routine until there was an opening to have the testing done. While lying still, face down in the machine, with the loudness overtaking my senses, despite soothing music in the background, I worked on keeping my mind in peaceful thought, and began making lists of things that I needed to get finished before the weekend. When it was over, more than thirty minutes later, I instantly felt like I was going to vomit as I sat myself up, which was similar to the feeling I always got during periods of motion sickness. I quickly dressed, found the closest bathroom, emptied my stomach of my lunch, and returned to work.

A call came later that afternoon and caught me off guard. I was asked to return the following day for a biopsy of my right breast. The scheduler wanted to move things along quickly because the MRI machines were scheduled for routine maintenance and if I were not able to go in the following day, then the next appointment would be ten days later, based on an already-full schedule. Although I shared this information with my husband, and we arranged for a switch in drop-off and pick-up duties for our son, I didn't let my family know about this new information, as I didn't want to worry them unless I felt it to be absolutely necessary. This was the same practice that I took during my thyroid debacle, and it wasn't until my parents stopped over to our home a day later for a quick visit and saw the neck bandage in place, one that I couldn't hide, that they found out about my abnormal testing and recent biopsy. The waiting game was becoming more difficult for me as a parent of a young child at home, but it was especially so for my parents who still had flashbacks of being told their daughter was ill seventeen years prior.

The scheduled breast biopsy was MRI-guided and didn't take very long. I was in and out of the women's breast health center within an hour and a half. I was also able to return to my normal daily activities later that afternoon. No one could tell that I had a bandage in place under my clothing, or that I was a bit sore with any sudden movement of my right arm. I let my mind drift again to the familiar place that it always returned to during scans, and I started to prepare for all possibilities, good and bad. When the final pathology results returned, and revealed atypical hyperplasia, a precancerous condition that describes an accumulation of abnormal cells in the breast—a potential forerunner to the development of breast cancer—I was then referred to a breast specialist.

I prepared myself for this visit by doing quite a bit of my own research on the risks associated with breast cancer in young adults following treatment for Hodgkin's lymphoma. I quickly learned that although Hodgkin's lymphoma cure and survival rates reflect some of the most successful in childhood cancer, the treatments, specifically radiotherapy, have increased the risk for secondary malignancies, with breast cancer being the most common after mantle radiation in young women. The incidence of breast cancer in women who received higher dose radiation, as I had, to the lymph nodes in the neck, chest, and arm pits, are estimated to have a risk of developing cancer twenty-four times higher than the average, and risk continues to persist even twenty to thirty years after the initial diagnosis, making mortality associated with breast cancer after childhood cancer substantial.

My initial consultation with the chief of surgery went better than I could have hoped for. After reviewing my extensive personal and family history, examining me, educating me on atypical hyperplasia of the breast, and finally discussing my already heightened risk of developing breast cancer due to radiation exposure, we reviewed all options, my preferences, and then decided together that pursuing an elective bilateral prophylactic mastectomy was in my best interest. I left the office that day with instructions to wait for a call from the scheduler regarding pre-admission testing as well as a referral to a plastic surgeon for initial consultation given the plan for reconstructive surgery. Once all of the scheduled consultations had taken place, and the times and dates were put on my calendar, I again had a feeling that I was beating the odds.

While discussing with my husband my decision to proceed with life-altering surgery, I came to realize quickly how supportive he was in terms of me doing what I felt was right for my mind and my body, without judgment. Known for being headstrong and fiercely independent, this was the approach from a partner that I needed to feel well cared for. A similar conversation with my parents did not go as well as I had anticipated. My dad remained quiet and simply nodded his head to most of what I had to say, but my mom questioned why I would consider putting myself through an estimated six- to eight-hour surgery, multiple-day hospitalization, six- to eight-week recovery, and future reconstructive surgery at such a young age, instead of considering a more conservative approach with ongoing frequent monitoring. Being a mother and a health care provider, I explained my preference to be proactive rather than reactive, weighing possible future risks and wanting to take as much control into my own hands as possible. I also dreaded such frequent testing due to the anxiety that it caused me multiple times a year. My closest friends voiced their support of this difficult decision and the role that they would help play in my recovery, which also made a world of difference to me.

In preparing for this upcoming surgery, I was referred to a young adult support group at the breast health center. Seeing as to how I had a fulfilling experience with my former teen support group, I was looking forward to taking part in the hour-long round table conversation. Ironically, it was also being held on a Friday evening. Introductions were made, and although I was surrounded by a strong presence of females from their mid-twenties to late thirties, I felt like the odd one out. Although each one of us shared the title of survivor, I was the only one at the table that evening who was choosing to have surgery without an active diagnosis of cancer. I could empathize with them for the struggles they were facing as parents, spouses, and employees, but with that empathy came guilt. Guilt of having the choice to proceed with surgery prior to the development of the enemy, also known as cancer. I let myself take in every last bit of information they were willing to share regarding what I may expect from the day of surgery to the end of my recovery, and I tucked it away, as I knew it would help me during my uncertain and long road ahead.

Surgery day had finally arrived and I kissed my now three-and-a-half-year-old blonde beauty goodbye for a few days. My husband accompanied me to the hospital, and as I expressed my concerns to him that surgery would be long and complicated, fearing the potential for a less-than-optimal outcome, he reminded me of my strength and remained positive and optimistic about my future. Several hours into the almost six I spent in the operating room, my dad arrived to be an extra layer of support and a lunch partner for him. I remember waking up in recovery, nauseous and in pain, seeing my husband and then parents, kissing them goodnight, and sending them home with instructions to rest and then allow me to do the same.

The next few days were a blur of post-operative haze, tolerating small advancements in eating, pain medication, going to the bathroom, and then dressing myself to go home. Fortunately, I was discharged within seventy-two hours without major complications, and tolerated everything as well as could be expected.

During the planning process, I elected to undergo skin-sparing mastectomies. With this type of surgery, all of the breast skin, except for the nipple and areola, is preserved. The breast tissue is removed through the opening that is created, and the remaining pouch of skin provides a good shape and form to accommodate an implant or a reconstruction using your own tissue. I underwent immediate breast reconstruction at the time of the mastectomies. The first stage of this reconstruction was the placement of tissue expanders, under the skin that was left. I awoke from surgery with two new scars, several drains, and the resemblance of breasts.

During my almost eight-week recovery phase, I couldn't drive at first, especially while requiring pain medication, and was restricted on lifting anything over the weight of a gallon of milk, which included my toddler who wanted to be picked up constantly. I returned home with two plastic drains left in, one on each side, that needed frequent attention, specifically to be emptied of their serosanguineous accumulations, and bandages that required changing. My husband became my nurse after putting in long hours at work and then extra time caring for our son. Surprisingly, he was highly skilled at manipulating those plastic drains and kept a straight face when cleaning my newly scarred areas and applying topical creams to help in the healing process.

I required frequent visits to the plastic surgeon to have the expanders slowly filled with saline over the next weeks to months, as tolerated, until I reached my desired size. Luckily for me, my dad still found joy in being my driver, and we spent many a morning grabbing coffee, a doughnut, and a talk while in route to my appointments. For me, this expansion process did not take as long as I had anticipated, because it was uncomfortable, and I decided to stop earlier and at a smaller size than I had originally planned. Approximately five months after that first surgery, I was scheduled to return to the operating room for the second stage and my final stage of reconstruction. The expanders were removed and replaced with implants. Recovery was quick and I felt like myself again. I could have then decided to proceed with reconstruction of the nipple and areola, sometimes done by skin grafting or tattoo ink, but after debating it, I made a personal choice to forgo both. The surgeries were a success, and I haven't regretted my decision to proceed with them even once.

CHAPTER 18

PALLIATIVE CARE

There have been several moments in my career as a palliative care physician assistant where I've been blindsided by a tidal wave of my own emotion while in the field providing patient care. There are two incidences that stand out amongst the many that can bring me to my knees if I let myself get caught up in the details.

I was part of the multidisciplinary care team for a thirty-something-year-old patient who presented to the hospital frequently with uncontrolled burdensome symptoms requiring prolonged hospitalizations, complicated by chronic pain, shortness of breath, weight loss, depression, and anxiety. As I looked further into the patient's history, I came to realize that there was a similarity between us, that of young adult cancer survivorship. During the patient's teenage years, she had been told that she was facing a potentially terminal illness, although different than my diagnosis. Her carefree days of attending school and extracurricular activities had also been stripped from her and replaced with multiple hospital visits, surgeries, chemotherapy, and radiation. She persevered just as I had, and beat the initial odds but not without roadblocks sneaking up on her along the way.

However, decades later, her body and her mind continued to be impacted by secondary complications related to the life-prolonging treatment she had received while fighting to survive. With that fight came limitations and what seemed to be never-ending complications. These limitations eventually contributed to her inability to hold a steady job, requiring her to file for medical disability. She had difficulty living independently, resulting in the eventual need for assistance with simple activities of daily living, first by visiting nursing staff at home. Subsequently, she required placement into a skilled nursing facility, as she was plagued with an altered body image, panic attacks, depression, and unrelenting physical and emotional pain and suffering.

During multiple encounters over the course of a year, while further exploring her story and listening attentively to and addressing her symptoms, and hearing her fears and goals for a meaningful existence, I was brought back to my own journey as a young adult cancer survivor. Although we started off so similarly, our paths had veered off from one another. Yes, secondary complications were a large part of each of our stories, but fortunately, I was able to manage my road blocks with reboots and relatively short recovery phases followed by a return to a demanding home and work life. My fellow young adult survivor was inundated with complications that could be linked back to treatments that had saved her life many years ago, but now only caused havoc.

Ultimately, with the support of her family and close friends, her goals of care became clearer over time and she asked to transition from active treatment of potentially reversible processes to active treatment of symptoms only for improved quality of life, voicing acceptance of a potentially limited life expectancy. The recurrent hospital admissions, frequent testing, and procedures had taken their toll on her with perceived limited benefits and an unacceptable quality of life.

Weeks later, she passed away surrounded by her loved ones, and I pray that she was finally at peace.

It was challenging for me, a provider on her medical team, to accept the real burdens and consequences that life-saving medical treatment had contributed to years later, and at the same time find the strength to grieve the loss of someone that could have very easily been me. Thoughts of guilt and sorrow came over me as I paid my respects to her family on the day of her services. Silently again, I vowed to myself that I would continue to live each day to the fullest and without regret, for time on this earth is truly a gift and our days are not guaranteed.

CHAPTER 19

ROLE REVERSAL/PAPA Z: FROM CAREGIVER TO CARE RECEIVER

As I swiped my badge to log on to a computer, in the middle of a busy station in the progressive care unit of the hospital, with the plan to look up information on a patient for whom a palliative care consult had been requested, I had to fight back tears as I glossed over the similarities between the patient and my father. And as I delved further into the background of this particular patient's chronic illnesses, which ultimately contributed to an unfavorable prognosis, I realized at that moment, that I could very easily be on the other end of the consultation I was about to give. Instead of the provider, I would be the devoted daughter of a very sick man. The emotion that came with that realization was almost too much to bear, and I needed to take five minutes to collect my thoughts and calm my nerves before returning to my task at hand.

The colorful and sometimes crazy man that was a constant by my side throughout my health care journey was now facing one of his own. Diagnosed during his young military years with ulcerative colitis, a chronic inflammatory bowel disease that causes inflammation and ulcers in the digestive tract, including the colon and rectum, he had become accustomed to routine medical appointments, scopes, and eventually long-standing daily medications to reduce his symptoms of abdominal pain and cramping, frequent diarrhea, rectal bleeding, anemia, and fatigue. At times, he was able to achieve long periods of remission and went about his life day by day, working long hours of overtime and never complaining or bringing much attention to himself, unless he had a common man cold.

About a year before this intense realization hit me, when his disease became debilitating despite ongoing medical management, I advocated for him to be referred to a tertiary care center and be evaluated for possible surgical intervention. During that visit, the well-respected surgeon went over his options, which included a total colectomy. This is a surgical procedure that removes the large intestine from the lowest part of the small intestine to the rectum, and an ileostomy would be formed to remove waste out of his body. This procedure would leave him with what my dad often referred to as "a bag," and if all went well, would require him to stay up to a week in the hospital. During the outlining of risks and complications, and after weighing benefits and burdens, I asked him what his thoughts were about his next steps. He tearfully told me that he would "rather die on the operating table while attempting to improve his quality of life, than to continue living in chronic pain and a state of hell." And just like that, his goals were clearly outlined for my family and I to follow.

Surgery was successful but complicated, and as my mother, sister, and I received direct word from the lead physician on his case, he confirmed the poor state of dad's colon. There was a new development of abdominal swelling caused by the accumulation of fluid, which in his condition was most likely related to liver disease. Another curve ball was thrown.

One of the rare life-threatening outcomes of ulcerative colitis is the development of primary sclerosing cholangitis, a disease of the bile ducts, which carry the digestive liquid bile from your liver to your small intestine. Chronic inflammation causes scarring to develop within the ducts, making the bile ducts narrow, which gradually can cause serious liver damage, cirrhosis of the liver with portal hypertension, and end-stage liver disease. In most people, the disease progresses slowly, and liver transplant is the only known cure.

Dad had a complicated post-operative course requiring an extensive hospitalization including quite a few setbacks, but eventually, almost three weeks later, he transitioned home and into his new life. He affectionately named his new appliance "Clyde" and had expertly learned how to manage his ostomy. He learned what foods he could eat and those he would now have to avoid. To us, he seemed perfect, like he always had, but to others who hadn't seen him in months, he looked like a new person. His face was drawn and discolored, he had aged years in the matter of months, and he appeared a shell of the strong man he once was. He looked chronically ill. I recall being at an event with him some months later and being asked, "Is your dad sick?" Our roles were reversed, as I'm sure my dad had faced that same question about his daughter many times.

During an early evening end-of-the-year musical performance put on at my son's school, my husband and I awaited the arrival of my parents in a very cramped and hot auditorium. As they arrived and I took one look at my dad, my heart instantly sank and I knew things were changing rapidly for our family. The whites of his eyes were yellow, and his skin resembled the color of a neon highlighter. I gave him a kiss on the cheek and an extra tight squeeze hello, and then quietly asked him for permission to call the liver specialist the next day.

My call led to an urgent evaluation followed by devastating news. Extensive testing confirmed what I had dreaded yet anticipated. He was one of the approximate 4 percent of patients with inflammatory bowel disease that developed primary sclerosing cholangitis. Given the severity of his disease and the rapid progression, discussions about a liver transplant were quickly initiated. The median length of survival from diagnosis to death is approximately twelve years, but prognosis is more dismal for those who are symptomatic at the time of diagnosis. And my dad was as symptomatic as those with similar advanced disease could become.

As my sister began researching her potential role in a living-donor liver transplant, I spoke to the liver team to see if this alternative was available at the center we had chosen, over waiting for a deceased-donor liver to become available. Because the human liver regenerates after surgical removal of part of the organ, and my sister was young and relatively healthy, she would have to undergo further testing, but could potentially be considered a good candidate. It was no doubt that it would be overly stressful to have both she and dad in surgery at the same time, and then facing their different recoveries—one as a single mom of a vibrant toddler and one as a sixty-six-year-old—but we were willing to do whatever was necessary to buy him some additional family time, as that is what he expressed he wanted. He was ready to put up one hell of a fight, just as I was all those years ago.

As my parents attended mandatory classes on liver transplantation, they continued to share their new information and their concerns with my sister and I. Our dad was quite vocal about not wanting his youngest daughter to have surgery on his behalf due to potential complications for her. He wanted both of us to live a long and healthy life and to be there for our children's milestones as he had been for each of us. He was interested in proceeding with additional specialty appointments and testing to allow him a spot on the deceased-donor liver transplant list. He decided to put his faith into God and his medical team to try to manage all they could until his name was called.

While attempting to remain a strong advocate for my dad by filling the same role he had held in my life, I was also trying to maintain the responsibilities that came with being a full-time mom, wife, and palliative care provider in the inpatient setting. I felt like I was being pulled in a million different directions constantly. The primary hospital caring for my dad's needs was almost ninety minutes away with traffic. This led to some very long days starting with school or daycare drop offs, work, and then the juggling of testing and procedures. Restful sleep was hard to come by. Free time was non-existent.

Amid this trying time, a day that I had been pouring my heart and soul into planning for almost a year was right around the corner. For National Cancer Survivors Day, I had invited my family and closest friends, amongst them those warriors from my teen support group days and their parents as well as members of my young adult survivor support group, to celebrate a special milestone with me. I was holding a fundraising event, in my favorite beach town, to celebrate my twentieth year of remission. Donations were being accepted for the Tomorrow Fund, the local nonprofit that had provided me and my family with financial and emotional support two decades earlier, to develop a grant to help young adult survivors get busy living! Money collected would be designated to assist with prescription copays, medical and mental health expenses, wellness goals, education, and family building through infertility and adoption services, all services close to my heart.

Because cancer is so costly, survivors face significant burdens once treatment is behind them, especially when they are young adults restarting their lives before they've even really had a chance to get them underway. And for all the blessings in my life, I felt the best way to celebrate my survivorship milestone was to give back by helping new warriors succeed in their quest to live a full life and make a difference.

I was expecting almost seventy guests, and despite my excitement to see everyone I cared about in one place, I considered canceling given my dad's unpredictable health. After much thought and just as many conversations about it with my core support group, it became clear that this event was just as important for my parents, and would go on just as we had initially planned.

Sunny skies, the smell of the ocean, big smiles, and lots of happy tears filled the afternoon of celebration. It was amazing to have my loved ones and strongest supporters surround me as my good friend and former pediatric oncology nurse practitioner took center stage to share information about childhood cancer research, the importance of longstanding survivorship screening, and life after cancer. As I made sure to capture the highlights with lots of photos being taken, little did I know that a picture captured of just me and my parents would be the last of its kind. As the afternoon came to a close and memories were imprinted on my heart and in my mind, my focus again shifted to the fight that was going to be my toughest one yet.

In order to be certain that my father's heart could withstand potential liver transplantation, an invasive surgery, he underwent cardiac testing, including an EKG, echocardiogram, and stress test. Although he had never been diagnosed with anything cardiac-related prior to this point, he carried a strong family history of heart disease with his dad dying in his early sixties of a fatal heart attack. An abnormal stress test led to a cardiac catheterization, a procedure where a catheter is inserted in an artery or vein in your groin, neck, or arm and threaded through your blood vessels to your heart to diagnose and treat cardiovascular conditions. It was with these results that our journey changed course.

Dad's catheterization revealed three-vessel disease. He was found to have diffuse cardiovascular disease with almost 90 percent blockages in two of the three major vessels; this was not considered amenable to intervention. With the plan for conservative cardiac medical management only, liver transplant was now off the table. He had also started to develop kidney disease. His organs were becoming more stressed by the day. And our time was getting short.

CHAPTER 20

FULL CIRCLE

Just two weeks after my survivorship celebration, dad ended up in the hospital with worsening liver and kidney failure complicated by a joint infection. His spirits lessened every day that he was cooped up in the sterile environment away from his favorite spot—sitting outside on his deck with the sun on his face. I was able to sneak him in Dunkin' Donuts coffee and jelly doughnuts on several occasions, which always brought a smile to his face. With some planning, we were able to get him home with my mom and sister taking on the role of caregivers; despite my mother's shaky hands, and my dad's military tone as he directed her how to properly hook up his antibiotics, things were going as well as could be expected.

Several weeks prior to his condition changing, I had begun interrogating my dad on his faith and asked if he had any interest in pastoral support as he faced a progressive illness and a limited future. His affirmative answer both surprised and pleased me, and I quickly outreached to the one person that I absolutely knew he would be able to connect with on a profound level. Dad had met Father at least seventeen years before, as he was the best friend of my West Coast boyfriend. He and I were the same age and had spent quite a bit of time together back in the day. I knew my dad would feel comfortable opening up to someone that he had a prior connection with and respected. I had given Father an update on his condition, and once dad returned home from the hospital, he graciously came to the house and met with him for prayer and support. Dad had shared with him that he believed he may have six months to live, and was welcoming and appreciative of ongoing spiritual support along his end-of-life journey. They left one another with plans to meet up again in the coming week.

While dad was in deep conversation and prayer, I connected with three of his close military friends and asked them to come visit that same Wednesday afternoon. The men spent several hours sitting and laughing together, eating lunch, and sharing old stories, something they were all good at doing. Later that afternoon, a hospice representative met dad and I at home. We signed on to the service with plans to focus on his quality of life and comfort, and to complete the course of antibiotics while maximizing support for him as the patient and for his immediate family, which included my mom, sister, nephew and grandmother living in the home.

Several hours after I had returned home and gotten into bed, the telephone rang. My mother and sister had called to say that my father had fallen in the bathroom, and he was bleeding from his ostomy bag.

Because they were unable to get him up and were concerned about possible injury, the paramedics were called and he was transported to the hospital to attempt to control the bleeding. By the time I arrived at the hospital less than an hour later to meet my sister and mother, labs had already been drawn in the emergency department and dad was found to be severely anemic and in kidney failure. It was close to midnight, and he opted to stay the night to receive blood products in an effort to optimize his condition and make him feel better. I requested a palliative care consultation for the next morning, and asked the medical team to alert the hospice team that he had been admitted for symptom control, but our preference was to discharge as soon as possible. As I walked my mother and sister out of the hospital, I tearfully told them to prepare for the end. Dad was dying.

Hours later, while by his bedside, I noticed the bleeding was faster than the blood products being administered. He was not a candidate for surgical intervention, and I knew the end was nearing. My parents, sister and I took a selfie together from his hospital bed. Given his increasing symptom burden and his desire for comfort in a private room setting, a decision was made to transition him to the inpatient hospice center that was just down the street. Our immediate family and closest friends were called and quickly surrounded his bedside, covering him in love while reminiscing about our most valued memories. You see, even as this was occurring, I truly don't believe that my dad thought he was dying. He ate lunch and dessert and graced us with his genuine smile and a twinkle in his tired eyes. Father was able to make it to the hospice center just as he became unresponsive. Dad was given the Sacrament of the Sick, and then we sang him his favorite song, "Jingle Bells." Not long after, he took his final breath, on July 3rd, and my life was forever changed.

We think there is always a tomorrow, so why expose our feelings today? Why risk being vulnerable? Why take the chance? Because today, what we love and what we feel, is what is real. Tomorrow it may all change.

EPILOGUE

"I Am"

I am a thirty-eight-year-old woman who appreciates life.

I still wonder when scientists are going to find a cure for cancer.

I encourage my son to try his best each and every day.

I pray the world will become a better and safer place.

I have worked hard to have a successful medical career.

I am a thirty-eight-year-old woman who appreciates life.

I no longer have to pretend that I'm as well as everyone else.

I feel my dad encouraging me from heaven with a firm hand on my shoulder.

I read a book, drink a coffee, or take a spin class when my attitude needs a lift.

I worry that I will continue to have late-effects from prior cancer treatments.

I am a wife, mother, daughter, sister, godmother and friend.

I am a thirty-eight-year-old woman who appreciates life.

I now understand that there is no such thing as perfect.

I strive to make a difference in the lives that I encounter.

I dream about helping survivors chase their tomorrow.

I am blessed to be alive.

I am still that courageous girl who appreciates life.

—KZM 2017

ACKNOWLEDGEMENTS

To My Readers- Thank you for reading my story and helping to support young adult survivors chase their tomorrow. Remember to embrace each moment and find the sunshine amongst the storm.

To Dad, Mom and Nik- Never ending love and thanks for advocating for my needs, being a shoulder to cry on, taking my swim cap off, and going without so I didn't have to.

To LPD and KG for being my biggest and loudest cheerleaders in the completion of this project.

To My Friends and Family-Thank you for standing by me throughout life's obstacles and helping to make each day brighter than the last.

To Cam – For giving me the blessing of motherhood and sleepless nights.

To Rick- For seeing the person behind the scars and loving her just the same.

The End

K. Zuba was raised in Rhode Island. She survived cancer as a high school student and currently works as a physician assistant specializing in palliative care.

Zuba and her husband, Rick, have a nine-year-old son named Cam. Outside of her work in the hospital, Zuba spends time watching Cam's soccer games, reading, and taking spin classes. She lives with her family in Massachusetts.

44976635R00073

Made in the USA
Middletown, DE
21 June 2017